Late Empire

Books by Lisa Olstein

Late Empire
Little Stranger
Lost Alphabet
Radio Crackling, Radio Gone

Late Empire
Lisa Olstein

Copper Canyon Press
Port Townsend, Washington

Front cover art: Erika Blumenfeld, *Light Recording: Dawn* (detail), 2008. Type 59 Polaroid Film. 5.25 × 4.25 inches. Back cover art: Erika Blumenfeld, *Light Recording: Dusk* (detail), 2008. Type 59 Polaroid Film. 5.25 × 4.25 inches. www.erikablumenfeld.com

Copper Canyon Press is in residence at Fort Worden State Park in Port Townsend, Washington, under the auspices of Centrum. Centrum is a gathering place for artists and creative thinkers from around the world, students of all ages and backgrounds, and audiences seeking extraordinary cultural enrichment.

LIBRARY OF CONGRESS CATALOGING-IN-PUBLICATION DATA
Names: Olstein, Lisa, 1972– author.
Title: Late empire / Lisa Olstein.
Description: Port Townsend, Washington : Copper Canyon Press, 2017.
Identifiers: LCCN 2017016315 | ISBN 9781556595189 (paperback)
Classification: LCC PS3615.L78 L37 2017 | DDC 813/.6—dc23
LC record available at https://lccn.loc.gov/2017016315

98765432 FIRST PRINTING

COPPER CANYON PRESS
Post Office Box 271
Port Townsend, Washington 98368
www.coppercanyonpress.org

Toby (for you)

Contents

◇

Late Empire

BUILT FOR IT

Maybe age or some other slow cooling
of the limbs one day will will me
from the water, from this desire to
plunge my body in. I tried hot yoga once,
once, winks the fireman on the park bench
overlooking the sea. To be honest, he says,
it felt like wearing full gear in a house fire.
You should try Bikram, says the mother
in workout clothes taking a sticker for her kid.
Whose motives are ever pure? Let's face it,
tennis is mostly about the outfits even if
it is what taught me how to go for the other
girl's jugular, that I should, even with her
daddy watching. Want rings out in the house
of the self and in the self the self must live.
It's Friday morning and I know what I'm doing
here, but what's everyone else's excuse?
There's everything and nothing to want
from the sea, the sea who does not answer.
Complete refusal transforms itself
into a kind of total acceptance, at least
so it seems because one way or another
our voices travel away from us and this is
a relief. Code Red, the children scream
every time they spy a crab. Dozens of men
are killed, says the paper, and their wives
are kept for single soldiers of the day's conquering.
Killed, we say, if a war zone. Kept, we say,
if a woman. Love–love we say when the score is
zero. Irrelevant, says the sea into which
everything we throw away ends up, words.

THIS IS OUR AMERICAN AMERICA HERE IS YOUR SON

We bring the world to bed with us,
its weather, its moving maps,
and its wars. When the staff told
the grieving chimp, tomorrow
they'd bring her a baby, she understood
her baby, the one three years ago
whisked inexplicably away,
not any baby, which is what
they brought. Of course
she wouldn't touch it. Of course
this lasted all day and into
the night and by morning
had been replaced by embrace.
Kinship is a gun set to stun,
circumstance a falcon striking
midair. Tonight I know the head
shot, I know the kneeling man.
If you know a face, when you
know a face, how you know
a face is the way every part of it
works together when, still a person,
across a table a person laughs
on just another sunny day.

ARRANGEMENTS

It's November, so we're talking politics
and I've been personally selected to hear
from Mark Ruffalo what it was he dreamt
last night. This is when I begin to imagine
his beautiful blurred head sinking into
and somehow floating above a pillow
very white and his beautiful blurred children,
but no, no thank you, no wife, because
if not here then where, exactly, am I
supposed to insert myself? And if we're talking
movie stars, Mark seems to be doing it right.
At least, anyone who still manages to be sexy
even when you know you're being played
must be the good kind of wrong. *Imagine,*
Mark writes. *Imagine,* is what he dreamt
last night, *imagine a world,* and then
I lost track of what he was so artfully made
to be saying, but dinner was involved
and a chance at something, a chance
for something, a chance. Mark, what if
by chance I met my true love when I was
too young to know to keep him? Mark,
what if by character or by foolishness
or by fate sometimes good people are
inexorably drawn to their own demise?
Marked by desire is usually code for something
catastrophic and even when we try to focus
with quiet minds and pursue the animal
feelings within us with only the most
measured sighs, so often something
catastrophic is what turns up in the late light
of early night, like you did on Annette Bening's
porch in that movie and even as a loser,
Mark, you were sexy, but less so, I'd be lying

if I didn't admit. Line, please. Just give me
a hint. Actually, let's take ten, I need
some time alone in my trailer. Sometimes,
we arrange in our minds a thousand goodbyes.
By arrangement, a funeral publicly can be
held to honor a body not present or, privately,
for somebody technically not dead yet.
Final arrangements may be made in advance
and locked in a drawer in a sealed envelope
with *to be opened in the event of my death*
scrawled elegantly across the seam.
Imagine, the next e-mail in my queue details
arrangements being made to honor a man
who made arrangements for the dispersal
of his modest assets by embedding subtle clues
only his family would detect in the arrangement
of the phrases of what turned out to be,
and probably he knew it, a farewell letter
his cellmate memorized the night before
his ransom came through. The cellmate's, Mark.
Like so many of the best parts of ourselves,
like so many of the characters we like to watch
you play, he was the good one left behind.

QUESTIONS ARE AN ATTRIBUTE OF GOD

Light a steeple bright enough and blind
the bats will come stitching white
against the torn black cloth of sky.
All these years and still no one knows
what draws the moths and their buzzing
relations with tired jaws, or at least
no one's told me. We know enough
to stop and look up, but not one thing
more. They look like manta rays
riding moony ocean waves, like lumens
let loose from a drunken ray gun.
I'm not necessarily convinced by ideas
that have been around so long it seems
their time must have come, but coyotes
do fill the night with tricks when they
throw their voices from bedside lamp
to rising sun, and reincarnation is one
explanation for some kinds of otherwise
inexplicable love. Forever my horse
has thought he is descended from unicorns,
he tells me over and over with the one
brown and one blue lake of his eyes
and doesn't bat a lash when I tell him
unicorns only ever inhabited brutally
the northernmost seas. He just champs
his bit a little and stamps any nearby puddle
and refuses to blink, as if to say, yeah
well, what's all that about you and whales
and the scaled digits of your precious thumbs?
On the 2× life-size statue of the saint
beneath the steeple beneath the moon,
the most realistic way to depict the eyes
is the inverse of true: pupils a bolt of stone
and all around them nothing but absence.

THE DISASTER

The disaster ruins everything.
There is no reaching the disaster
this way, the disaster threatens.
The disaster is separate, the disaster
does not come. We suspect the disaster
is thought. To think the disaster,
we are on the edge of disaster
already. When it comes upon us
the disaster is imminence: disaster
detached from the disaster. Time
belongs to the disaster. The disaster
has always already withdrawn,
there is no future for the disaster.
The disaster is perhaps related to
forgetfulness, the disaster not thought—
not knowledge of the disaster,
knowledge disastrously. The disaster
is perhaps passivity. Night, white
sleepless night, such is the disaster,
night lacking darkness, night separated
from star. The disaster exposes us
with respect to the disaster. Nothing
suffices. The disaster would liberate us
if it could. The disaster does not
impose itself. The disaster is not
our affair. The disaster takes care
of everything.

NIGHT PEOPLE

Your legs like a dog's run in sleep
through made-up meadows.
Every breath borrowed, every breath
owed. We've been going about it
the wrong way: kissing with our mouths
full of rings, trying to read the future
in the prism cut of snow. No amount
of calling means someone's there
not answering on the other end of the line.
No amount of belief or disbelief keeps
the plane from falling from the sky.
All around the world we light up
like stars, like searchlights, like
the map of the earth we actually are.
We talk about talking: this sensor
to that satellite, a ping, a blip,
an uneventful goodnight. We think
about thinking: how distances are
calculated, how long the mind
of a machine might hum. Malaysia
then is everywhere tonight's meadow
of sleep or no sleep, of dark waves
cradling dreams of flying. Tonight
we are all Malaysia Airlines
as we like to say, as we have learned
to say, as it somehow comforts us
to say. Tonight, this week, for as long as
we can bear it or until something
pulls us away we are all one hundred
and fifty-three Chinese nationals and
six Australians and three
Americans—and it doesn't feel to us,
and we are very rational girlfriends
who also happen to be scientists,

that they're gone—and twenty men
who worked for a weapons manufacturer
and the Defense Minister who is also
acting Prime Minister and the mainland
army night watchmen dozing in front of
their radar screens. We are all kissing
something dark tonight, in the dark
tonight, with our words or no words
but we are going about it the wrong way.

WHAT WE'RE TRYING TO DO IS CREATE A COMMUNITY OF DREAMERS

Horses, airplanes, red cars,
running. The Japanese sleep
less but do they dream less?
What do women in Stockholm
dream about in wintertime?
Show me every car dream.
Show me every car dream
in Moscow. Show me every
red-car dream that involved
men living in Las Vegas.
Compare that to Tokyo or Paris.
Do famous people dream
differently? If you have
more money in the bank?
Can we run an algorithm,
can we quantify, can we teach
that? The distance widens
and narrows, sometimes
a grapefruit, sometimes
a beach ball. Invisible data.
They say Einstein came up
with relativity in a dream.
What if you could go back
and find it?

WE LOOK FORWARD TO SEEING YOU AGAIN SOON

Maestro, meet me in the dark.
The truth is we prefer it this way,
stumble-gay and keening, I mean
preening, like the black-tongued
parrots on permanent display.
Herman the Giant German
Rabbit suffers exactly one fool
per day, the smiling silver one
bringing him food on a scuffed
aluminum tray. Past a certain age,
you don't ask a woman how she does
her hair no matter how elaborate
the braid. Straight queens and dry
drunks, fellow former future kings,
the gerbils of Kazakhstan—desert
rats, in point of fact—have something
to tell us about death riding shotgun
in our subway cars. Life is always
left-handed. Sleeping bees are
immobile bees whose bodies and legs
hang in the direction of gravity.
Lucky ones who find homes,
don't expect the left-behind to
thank you for remembering.

IT ALL LIGHTS UP

It's hard to feel spry in any room
they've pushed you in or out of
as if the walls remember the wheels,
their muted whine, and your own
whimpering cries as rosy-fingered dawn
licked you clean with her rough tongue.
We're all going to die, you've heard
a thousand times from your own
mother's mouth. You never believed her,
how could you, she invented life,
but then one day stuck in traffic
you catch yourself muttering the line
and it sticks and every stupid argument
comes back to you stupider still
and your petty feelings about the special
Employee of the Month parking space
and all those nights you settled
for takeout and a blindfold. Here
at the university, the corridors are
labeled Corridor. The visualization
laboratory is dark. Inside, scanning for
shark-shaped shadows, the surfer knows
to borrow the seal's suit is to borrow
its nightmares, too. Maybe today
species are outdated modes of technology,
and this is why we give them up
so easily. Sometimes there's a glitch
in the system. Fatal errors occur.

POSSIBILITY OF REPAIR

Now we grieve waving fuzzy
avatars in the clotted air, virtual
mourners lining up to testify to
a glimpse of a wisp of your hair.
A bunch of phonies, you might say,
where were you when the fox got
stumbling drunk on mulberry wine,
when the cat caught and released
that woodpecker onto the crooked
ladder of my spine? Ham and
cheese on a hillock where before us
Mohawks and mountain lions
and countless freshmen and maybe
a few freedmen once sled. Some
soggy children, a lost Spiritualist
or two, late to the orgy, their donkey
having taken a wrong turn early on,
but you know what they say about
all paths winding up the same hill.
Overcomplicated, the hooks and latches
on this brassiere, by which I mean
embrace. Beloved nobodies, deranged
neighbors, doppelgängers every one,
who among us is willing to look
with proper awe at the gossamer fawn
newly pushed from its flesh palace
into the wrong season's brisk air?
Snowflake, turn out that blue light.
Somehow we've ended up in the yard
again counting turkeys by hindsight.
Saintly, they'll be martyred beneath
the paling sun. Come on, we whisper
to the near disappeared. Come on,

come out, come up. Okay then, we say,
go on, some boats are made for one.

THE MESSENGERS COME WHEN YOU ARE SITTING AT THE TABLE

The heart of the head-cage rattles.
The front windows. The door.
Mean-drunk pilot, enraged
backseat driver, coked-out conductor
speeding through signals meant for
lesser trains, how can I help you,
what have you come here for?
Spirit recently ascended, hover
awhile above me. Soften my sky
with your gentle rain, the invisible
indivisible kind, droplets willing
to wet all parts of us. Spirit,
I hear before you rose up you were
on your way. I hear you said
great men eat a little bit of shit
every day. I see you turning parable.
I see you turning prank. I'd rather
have you down here, but it's true,
this other lasts longer. Go ahead,
claim to be Jewish, claim to be
a galaxy, go on gathering tribes
of sons and of suns. Technically,
says the boy lying still on his mother's
hard sofa, right now I'm flying
through space. Technically, the man
lying still on the soft bed of a new
grave is orbiting at an equal pace.
Mothers, he says, there's nothing
wrong with your sons. We're all fighting
for our lives. We all win for a while
and then we're done.

BLUE WATER NAVY

Darling, the world, it will come at you
with the migrating eyes of flounder
traveling through the matter of their own heads,
having reimagined axis and ground.
There is a certain parasite that turns a crab
from male to female, or is it female to male?
The average male armadillo's penis is larger
than that of some gorillas. I can't help it
if most facts are, in fact, facts about sex.
Don't bother pretending; don't try to
fix this for me. We *acquire* debt.
An animal is *able* to live in captivity,
which is where we take our measurements.
Watching them go at it sometimes we like to
say outgunned, outmanned, but definitely
not *outfought.* What we like is the idea
of making the invisible visible. True love
takes a lifetime of research. The foot
of the lake meets the mouth of the river.

AIR RIGHTS

One way to think of it is
I require absence and you are
lifelong a room just left. Except
you bloom not empty half-light
but a stand of trees at the edge
of the meadow where my life
leaks out. Static is the soundtrack
of the cabbie's dream but oh
how we love our troubadours,
sad acoustic boys and girls,
sunshine stuck in their throats. Some
days it takes all my concentration
not to pick the lettuce that lives
down the street. Then I wake
with tendrils between my fingers
and once again I'm feigning
innocence on the one hand,
aping grief on the other. See,
I would eat the lily from under
the frog, drink the river between
each strider's wake. It's my way
of feeling productive, of not
too terribly envying the swan
still as a figurine on her cloud mirror
until the trees go back to normal,
which is a kind of sleep instead of
clawing magnificent at the sky.

I WANT TO SAVE THIS WHALE

The one right in front of me
on e-mail, a chain message
forwarded by my mother
on the first day of this new year.
She's tangled in nets and lines
and there's only one way to
get her out, she tells us
with her bathtub-sized eyes
one at a time because we
have to swim around to see.

TURNED BACK THE DISASTER COMES BACK

Contrary, besieged, my self
makes me its accomplice.
I owe him, my mandatory proxy,
a borrowed happenstance,
a philosophy in place of me.
Welcome, difficult neighbor,
the patient, dying, announces,
for he is my neighbor, who
assigns the me in me eaten away.
Such is the new future no present
remembers: the fall of the regular
fall of the beat—the disaster
again. Speaking, we cause it
to appear, the gentlest want,
the same word crushed, feverish.
The disaster is beyond the pale.
Improper disaster, what have you
done? God no longer the neighbor
in this night spared. It is dark, disaster.
What a long way there is to go.

COLD COMFORT

Weather, whistle me this.
Soon you're all we'll talk about—
not in the old way, no longer
idle, but driving. Sure, we can
bury ourselves under a volcano
to simulate life on Mars
but the drill we run there
to test our ability to survive is
"my dog died." Often it seems
we find ourselves in another
world. Often when we find
our way it happens in a moment.
Then we live to do it again.
Occasional divers are hesitant.
I tend to swerve with the knife.
Don't you? Depraved heart,
this is where we stitch you up,
this is where we let you seam.
Most often it's you that fails us,
never supposed to beat so long.

NOTHING GOOD GETS AWAY

Shitty little mockingbird
on the parking lot cellphone
tower, we'll take it, your flashes
of bright white. We know all about
bowers and their blue obsessions,
crows and their shiny. There's
a girl flickering across the news
some murder brings presents to.

She's not dead, she's not even sick
yet. Arrow hugging sign-pocked
rooflines, once upon a forest
we modeled trajectory on your
shooting flight, then we positioned
our guns to put you in our sights.

LAKE EFFECT

Then I was a safe house for nothing.
The ear turns off with a click like a switch.
America, 22% of your highway drivers
are high. On the back roads, there's no telling
how many. Once I lived across from a long line
of dairy cows: they were stalwart in winter,
black and white come coyote, come snow.
I miss my friends especially in the dark.

Sometimes we slept under one roof. Sometimes
we shared a roof that was one cast of flood
threat or storm squall spread across the valley
like a parachute just barely billowing above
the ground. Nothing to see, nothing to hear.
No one in harness, but no one missing, either.

IMPLY A FUTURE

Abundance shames us differently
than want. Want fills us more
often than not. Knots are a science,
an art form, a mess. Is this one strong
enough for the big mean world?
Shut up, beautiful past, coffeecake
mornings overlooking the seal-less bay.
Shut up with your barking,

with your flagrant shark-calling ways,
future-furred mammals all doglike
and wide-eyed bobbing now
on the gentle waves. I wanted to
think of you in coves of absence
not wake to you in any real light of day.

MY LIFE BLEW UPON

Then I was a safe house for
morning. Outside bruised dawn.
We said it was a leopard
who did this to us. We said
the leopard had come and gone.
Then around us safe-like
the house clicked shut.
Love in action,

how different from love
in dreams. Intercellular
versus atmospheric. Fences
that collect the wind's garbage
versus mountains where
god crumpled the seam.

A HUNDRED THOUSAND QUESTIONS WHY

There is a long ditch in the village
of My Lai. You make of it a monument,
a love letter, a poem. You make of it
a housecoat with oversize pockets
perfect for stones. *My darling,*
no one was happier than we two
traffics by on the altared freeway
of the six-lane mind. Rubies come

bedded in Earth's best sea-foam.
Glittering contradictions of might.
You can't bomb knowledge, but
schools are a start. First the village,
then the river. Later on in the textbooks
that hum us to sleep at night.

HERD FLOCK HIVE

Threat gets our attention. Try
reading it again with a fever.
Try with a knife to your throat,
an oyster. Caught in the headlights'
glare the hare zigzags back
and forth to escape its own shadow.
Crickets come programmed
for evasive action: first,

move left; second, move right;
beyond that there's no predicting.
Nights, we take nothing to our breasts.
Ghost milk slakes ghost thirst.
Every one of its hundred blue eyes
tells the scallop when to slam shut.

WAITING FOR YOU TO SPEAK I MOUTH THE WORDS

Then I was a safe house for
what, the weather, that mother,
this catchall we call you? When
the sun is shining. When the clouds.
Apparently for something we are
searching because what else is this
constant looking looking for? Is it
like this for any or all the small

animals dumbstruck by cold
as they go about their gathering,
their putting on of fat and fur?
Do they know *what for* the way
they know *what to*? What to do?
Stay alive. What for? For you.

FALLBACK POSITION

Unmoored, unnoticed: who hasn't
wondered how long she might go
unmissed by the remiss, who hasn't
called to mind that toddler suckling
her dead mother's tit? Call it a beautiful
travesty, the parking lot filled with elephants
milling about in hundred-degree heat
on concrete all day across from the air-

conditioned arena where each night
for a week they'll perform to a sold-out
crowd and of how we look forward to seeing
our favorite, the littlest one, on our way
each day, let us sing, as we might say
in worship or, we enjoyed you.

GOOD DEEDS UNDONE

Then I was a safe house
for every one of your bad dreams.
Not really, just a few. Just a drop
of poison, a poison pen, just
evermore dusky postpartum
between us two, each day
a portrait drawn of what I
couldn't do. My muse is not

a horse, but river necks craned
from behind stall doors or milling
quiet in a pen is how we like them,
thrumming center of space
defined, speed defied, all almost
and maybe, all someday and soon.

WE MOURN THE END BY APPLAUDING

It was something like a dream:
I looked for you and I looked
much too long. Something
like when a train blows steam enough
to call the clouds down. We pay
great chefs to concoct memories
for us, to make us recall what once
we something like were, or had,

but foamed air only reminds us
you can't eat nothing and expect to
sleep through the night. Summer once
shone lemon through your hair. When
I close my eyes I can make it back to
the barn but where have the horses gone?

WRONG QUESTION

Then I was a safe house
for the problem that chose me.
Like pure math, my results
were useless for industry:
not a clear constellation,
a scattered cluster, a bound
gap. When I looked I found
an explorer bent. Love

never dies a natural death.
It happens in a moment.
Everything hinges on
a delicate understanding.
Even the most trusted caregiver
is only trusted for so long.

PRIVATE DICK

One case from the past is
cause for particular vexation.
I must have done something
terribly wrong. To what end,
however? An object under
the hero's gaze falls to pieces
in your hands. Spirited through
time, riven, we make our meek

adjustments. There were many
occasions on which I arrived too
late. Strangled in fog, I offered
logic in return. I had meant to
wear a white shift, to slip back
into the crowd, to be stopped.

THE RESEMBLANCE OF THE ENZYMES OF GRASSES TO THOSE OF WHALES IS A FAMILY RESEMBLANCE

This world, Whistle, there's nothing for it, what can we possibly say? Cumulus sails and their endless blue ocean are a thin skin when viewed from space. Back home astronauts turn to drink or religion to shield the eyes, to cloud the vision— something was irreparable in the darkness or the largeness or the smallness they saw. This morning I watched two elephants dance the boogie-woogie. One added grace notes with its trunk, nodding its head in cool time. The other—half in, half out of the frame—shook its booty just like my friend, the best singer you'll ever never hear because for her the stage turned into a kind of prison, like the refuge, maybe, staffed by good people who wondered how the elephants would respond to the piano's rollicking tune, or who knew how and couldn't wait to watch them move. This morning, these last few days have been kissed with crisp in a benevolent air kind of way. It's spring and birds are busy and there's a mulberry tree popping berries and the city sings in distant sirens and steady traffic thrum. Soon the sun will burn too terribly strong again and the drought we're presently forgetting will press back into view against the bleached rocks that line the reservoir down which the water continues to crawl. This winter, up north the far north reached too far south. Here, more than three hundred million trees have died since our current thirst began. It's impossible not to feel thirsty, Whistle, under a sky like this. When a dead tree falls, a young, new tree will eventually grow in its place, a man named Burl who works for the forestry service reminds us, trying to be encouraging. I don't mean to be discouraging. It's beautiful here. It's just that fear has us in its thrall. Things are different or they're just like they've always been—we're not sure and we're not sure which is worse. We love it when animals act like us. I mean, just look at those elephants dancing. We see it as a kind of evidence, but maybe it's better for them to be nothing like us at all. They stop everything to mourn their dead. When choosing a direction, they engage in extensive debate. Rage follows cause. Whistle, they know when even a distant friend falls.

IT'S ANOTHER DEADLY DAY

Stepping thoughtless from the curb the dead bird was a bouquet at my feet, feather-fringed meat for not even a night scavenger's hunger. The sad truth is when it comes to protection or the casting of spells, the only viable solution to the madman is to hope he selects another according to what flies through the tunnel of his need: a length of hair or a cascade of chemicals on a given day combined with the mystery of traffic. This is no way to raise a daughter, Whistle, or oneself, up off the knees. Blond and thirty, seen it all day, a panhandler wearily indicts my friend stepping from the train into night rounds on the cancer ward. Part of what's hard is the constant beeping, she says, and we've made that true now everywhere, machines calling out coded bridges between the heart of some need and the ears of their masters, as if through their wiring now wireless, they could reach everything at once and keep us all in mind, and in a way they do. Today on a bird walk, Whistle, at the wastewater treatment plant, the vermilion flycatcher was our man overboard, our rose lost at sea. All around, the foliage explained how we come back from a freeze but we come back ugly: years of scarring measure one night's thick fist. *Melancholy,* sings the mockingbird, *Terror.* Nothing is ever the same.

SAD PROMOTION

Suddenly, Whistle, we wake to a flood of it, waves of data from all directions, and given the years and years of silence well beyond reasonable doubt, it's not unreasonable to wonder what new manipulation this sudden rush of information might be. As Kurt Cobain, a pain-shredded singer from my youth, before he blew off his head in a room over a garage adjacent to a lovely house he owned and when he did the radio station I favored broadcast his voice for twenty-four hours straight, supposedly said, just because you're paranoid doesn't mean they're not out to get you. In a few months, Whistle, I'll speak to a large room full of inspired speakers, and in part I will discuss the powers that both of our trainings in language, different though they may be, prepare us to apprehend and to deploy. Each in our own way, Whistle, we are in love with language and information and results and with verdicts, too—me, too, if I'm being honest. Busy and important and depended upon each of us plows the field of our day. Our obligations, Whistle, are impossibly too many and possibly too few. Don't bite off more than you can chew. Love what you do. There is so much we like to think we choose. Some people believe we are born again and again and that even this is a kind of decision we make. A time of catastrophe provides an opportunity for the acceleration of spiritual growth, is one take on the matter. That fear isn't only an echo from the past but the future calling, is another. Maybe then this trembling, Whistle, is both someone else's and my own. I sensed a great sadness in the air over the entire block, writes my friend upon returning home from the protest, a great sadness in the air.

TO THE LEFT OF BOOM

For days, the world breaks down into a series of scenes: at the spring-fed pool on Mother's Day, in the produce aisle, at the ball game, golden-lit, the about-to-be shattered, already doomed normal before the monster or the monster wave hits—sunshine on the canoe and glinting off the water smooth inches from the falls, innocently making a salad or taking a shower. It feels like a play today, Whistle, or like a shard of the future has lodged itself in my shoulder. Monday it's a report on the impossible future of bananas. Tuesday it's the story of limes held hostage by cartels. Both still appear on our shelves, but we don't know for how long. News comes and goes, but fate is a cycle longer to unfold. The fact is, we turn and turn away. Today the world is here for us with heart-shaped peaches ripening in a brown paper bag. There's no way to repay borrowed time, Whistle, so we spend it.

SPACE RACE

A city being built up, Whistle, looks a lot like a city being torn down—scaffolding and buckets, brick-sewn seams, dust clouds speckling the air. I'm planting a garden of all native species, but even it begins to feel like a zoo, a private parade of favored specimens. The rare pomegranate looks like the common carnation. Purple martins in fancy houses live with parasitic sparrows in their midst. It's the cost of doing business, because chasing them away takes all day. The days, Whistle, as someday you'll no doubt find out, are often tedious, circular corridors punctuated by doors opening onto small rushes of pleasure or pain, but in the end endless feeling, which is both a comfort and a source of despair, and either way an illusion we can't help but believe and know to be false at the very same time. So it's hard, Whistle, to keep the important questions in mind. A near miss reminds us: pulses drumming in our ears, tingling in every finger. What am I doing with my one little chance to be alive? my friend now distant sings through the car stereo I've put on because I miss her. Whistle, today they say the ocean will be empty in a future not too distant to imagine. There is a balancing act you will one day be introduced to and then never be free to unlearn, between the concerns of the day and the concerns of what we call the bigger picture. A friend of my friend who was paralyzed in a crash devotes herself to the cause of raising awareness about the small hard or even semisoft objects of daily use that can become deadly projectiles under the right conditions and I have no doubt she is correct, she is in fact expert, she is all the proof she needs, but who among us can bring ourselves to batten down every small thing to some not even invented yet small hatch like an astronaut patiently securing his rounded utensils in the womb of a capsule hurtling through space? We have no choice but to pick and choose, Whistle, yet this same equation is what will open our eyes to a lifeless ocean in fifty years, maybe sooner, according to today's news we can't bear to read. Instead we take quizzes about our personalities and our character traits, such as which marine animal are you?

NOW LEAD ME OUT OF THIS STORY, SPIRIT

The truth is, our regular problems are enough to fill the day. They occupy us completely. Just this week more than two hundred and fifty schoolgirls were kidnapped at gunpoint and at gunpoint forced to wed. Prayer was just allowed at Town Meeting in America and though this might not sound dangerous, it is a kind of torch to the house we dreamed we built. Scars and burns. Psoriasis. Epidemics of all kinds. Whistle, we have no idea how worried to be about the unforeseen effects of scientists in corporate laboratories shuffling the DNA of our food, but we know enough to be terrified of the master they serve. *Master* is at once a horrific and a hallowed word in our lexicon, Whistle. Maybe it's one we should never use again. Master class, master lock, master key, master cleanse, master of ceremonies, master of his domain, mastery. Lucid dreaming is a technique to gain mastery over dreams. I've had dreams, Whistle, since I was a child, of Nazis coming to our neighborhood, of them standing in the street below our windows on the evening before the day they will take us or everything we own away. The near-before, the pivot point between having and not having. Still having, having it taken from your very hands, Whistle, or having no choice but to watch it, to let it, go is exactly the moment most painful in the dream, which is always a bit different, but mostly the same: footsteps, long dark heavy coats, a chaos of choosing, belongings thrown from windows, but never the night inside the apartment, the hours there left to live.

A SIMPLE LESSON ON THE BURIED SPIRIT

This morning, Whistle, I overheard a man say on what could only be some kind of an audition, if you ask me do I believe in a power, yes, but it's not some old guy with his hand on the joystick and if you want to call that god, sure. The woman he was talking to nodded and said nothing and one day, Whistle, we will ask you what you believe, but this is a dirty trick because really all any of us has to believe in is what we've been taught. On a hilltop in Galilee a red heifer is guarded around the clock and her burnt-orange coat every day is parsed with a fine-toothed comb while several pairs of sanctified eyes scour the plains, the hills and valleys of her body searching for what they hope desperately never to find. Among my peers, there are parents who believe that the new generation, the one we're giving birth to, will arrive specially equipped to save us and Whistle, I sympathize, but this seems the dirtiest trick. We've lost the eyes of god, so don't look now but we're looking at you. I used to read mention of the poem in a poem as a self-aggrandizing gesture, but now I feel it as an admission of guilt. Every butterfly in this conservatory I escape to was raised by hand to die on the altar of our enjoyment or each lived a charmed and protected life in these hallowed halls, a perfect melting pot, an ideal microcosm under a protective dome as on the moon or Mars or wherever we may one day soon be heading. Today I stopped reading, Whistle, but I lingered to look at a picture of a full-grown Siberian tiger, three hundred and seventy-five pounds, bowing its head and placing the enormous pink palm of its paw to the tiny pink palm of a toddler pressed to a pane of zoo glass. Innocence to innocence, a benediction, forgiveness, a warning? It bowed its head and pressed its paw and rubbed its cheek against the glass in front of the little girl's face before turning away, an animal in some places believed to be

son of the same mother as man, in some places worshipped
as a god, an animal smart enough to hunt us not for meat but
for vengeance, Whistle, if given the chance.

OTHER THINGS IN VIEW

Often it's like a dream and we're stuck, the water's rising and we're running laps on a shrinking track. Just look at you, Whistle. Soon the beautiful, terrible demands of the day will break the hours around you into waves, no horizon in the distance and only occasionally the amnesia of deep sleep, otherwise a half-waking half-life that keeps all eyes trained on the next set of hurdles, on the stupid stopwatch. In other words, too often keeping afloat is all we can do. My friend does the math in her head, says what are we talking about, will our children have no children? and Whistle, she means you. We mean we know already nestled in the pockets of all the bodies are millions more, each of us a slippery bridge across we don't know what crossing soon foreclosed. From this position, Whistle, it seems everything has been a mistake. We ate when we were hungry. When we were forced to flee, we fled. Old movies look silly to us now and we wonder whether ever anyone sat in the velvet dark staring up and thinking the giant jerking puppets and the women and children screaming beneath them looked lifelike, like life. This week the twenty-ninth Godzilla movie will be released. Now we like the monster to mirror not just our fears but the fears that are our fault.

THE INVENTION OF PERSPECTIVE

To get on with the business of making a life, my body put up stores as if for a long winter. It changed me, Whistle, as it should, and still I keep the evidence close. The chemical composition of human milk is case-specific, sugars and fats, proteins tailored to the moment at hand and the mouth. The temperature of the human chest, if it is a mother's with her infant upon it, will rise or fall by as many as ten degrees as required for regulation. A young nursing mother once kept seven men and one baby alive with her milk for three weeks on a broken raft on the skin of the sea, a journey of hope gone awry and in the end they did endure a kind of safe passage to the dreamed-of shore from which they were promptly sent back. Safe passage is what we hope for and what we call a journey we survive. Passing we reserve for the dying, passed for the newly dead whom we wish safe passage to we don't know where. If we all painted our rooftops white, my friend says, it would be like erasing an entire year's harm. In the mind of a think tank lives the idea of a highway that powers the cars that drive it. The oldest maps are small wooden sculptures, Whistle, hand-carved, hand-smoothed, nut-brown, palm-sized replicas of the islands they describe from a distance of sea. The way they work is from something like a skin kayak or a dugout canoe, by turns you gaze out at the mist-veiled land rising across the waves and at its mirror in your hand and safely choose where to go or remember how to return.

A CRUCIAL ERROR

Drowning is silent, Whistle, a rash of new billboards around the city warns us. Along the way we learned the wrong lesson or we learned the lesson wrong. We believe in splashing and thrashing, something awful but at least kind of grand in its demand for our attention. A drowning person will pull you under, we've long been horrified to know and I'm not sure that's still true, but alone out there or silently in our midst it's a quiet barely bobbing of the head, a sinking and a fruitless not quite lifting of the face we must fear. So much right now seems metaphorical but they mean this literally. At the creek today wading away from the happy dogs in neon canine flotation devices paddling after neon balls, in a thicket of murk a few feet from my feet I saw a red life jacket pinned between current and rock and I was too scared to say anything or to reach out. It had been there for a long time, or at least long enough. There was no thrashing, no bobbing. No one was missing from the festive shore, no one was looking for anyone, at least not anymore. A friend I grew up with, Whistle, was broken not by watching the truck wreck her sister but by the house she lived in ever after lined with pictures her parents blew up and framed and framed. There is a man who after many years of practice has found a way to cut a perfect hole in a perfect ceiling to give us back the sky in ways we didn't realize we'd lost or maybe never knew. For a million dollars he will install one for you and through many meticulous calculations frame a god's eye or a god's-eye view, a kind of empty nest from which you turn your gaze skyward to a floating egg, maybe gray, maybe blue, or almost any color at all if you watch during the sunset light sequence he installs to show you exactly how much to believe your own eyes. Maybe if everything is relative, Whistle, then everything in its moment is absolute.

ESSAY MEANS TO TRY

A golf course, a prison, a wastewater treatment plant, six gas stations, a dollar store, a BBQ-Beer-Barbershop, two Baptist churches, one megachurch with a neon sign that flashes, *What's Missing In C-H - - C-H? UR!*, a Quaker meeting house, a women's and children's shelter, which I don't think is supposed to have a sign, Whistle, so the women and children might actually be safe inside, and signs for the Department of Corrections and the Department of Sanitation and the Department of Family and Children Services, and, for three days, a small hunched falcon on the west wire above the paved washout labeled Walnut Creek, and dozens of brittle lawns are what I drive by on my way to and from each day, Whistle, lately crying. My friend who has had the shutters slam closed too many times around her says, if you've been crying for more than two weeks already, you may need help to stop. And my almost friend except he scares me says, this is exactly what Empire wants you to do, sit around crying or sit around writing, playing the small-time artist-agitator role. Already during these two weeks of crying I've purchased seven books, each of which felt important to own, and taken one hundred and forty vitamins and filled three prescriptions, none to help with the crying. I've waited patiently or impatiently in countless lines, Whistle, sometimes crying; I've waited for news of loved ones such as you. Crying is how we enter the world, Whistle. We all come by sea, we all come by storm, we all tear apart and are torn.

DESPAIR FIRE

Whistle, today I sat in a crowded room and listened to children accompany one another to the songs of their parents' youth. We wept and we cheered and we were relieved when it was over. Nothing is uglier than a parent's anger at her child, nothing floods a person quite like the terrible tenderness, the desperate hope that he be spared. Later, my mouth was full of chocolate when I cried out alone in the car upon hearing the hostage's father explain that for all the years of his son's captivity, he lived according to the captors' time, waking, eating, sighing, sleeping out of sync with everyone around him as a way to stay connected, or maybe it was a form of distraction, the way my friend teaches terrified children to put their ears in the water by getting them to say *aloha* and other silly-sounding Hawaiian words or maybe the Hawaiian words are to distract him during the endless hours in the pale, lifeless pool or maybe they remind him of the blue sea day he knew he wanted to devote his life to water, which he does, but not in the way he imagined. The father's son has come back, Whistle, but not in the way he imagined. Guilty, was the verdict reached in the trial held by stolen candlelight in a court of starvation and depravation over a series of Auschwitz nights. God is guilty as charged, they said, then, let us pray.

EVERY PASTORAL IS AN ELEGY

Once I flipped, Whistle, over the front of a horse I was riding. He balked, pulled up, and above his dappled gray shoulder I sailed to the sawdust floor, belly up and tucked neatly beneath his raised razored hooves. Whistle, he stopped, miraculous in midair, in midstep, in microseconds, with great force of will and greater strain of muscle he refused something physics ordained, something for which he could bear no blame, like a god he interrupted cruel fate on my behalf. Later, from his back I spied in his turnout a perfect woven cup, a swallow's nest of hair plucked from mane or tail. Our bodies, Whistle, are the material of essential matters we can't foresee. If an alien in a galaxy sixty-five million light-years away is looking at us through a telescope right now it's looking at dinosaurs, says an astronomer on the radio on the anniversary of a famous stargazer's death. It's simple, he says, the reason we find no evidence of life-forms like us is they too quickly destroy their planets. Which animals do you think keep us company, my friend asks, in past and future knowing? Maybe whales, I say, maybe elephants, but we've already talked too much about sadness today and birds can know only the present tense of their flying we agree and agree to leave it there. Pigeons scour the sidewalk, grackles scour the air. Relief after rainstorms. Some days even business as usual feels rare. If you watch to the end, the amateur videographer says in a post below the movie he took of himself saving a fawn stuck between the metal bars of a neighborhood fence, it almost looks like the mother is thanking us. I saw it happen, Whistle, what the billboards describe, I saw it begin, a noiseless slipping of the face beneath the surface, the silence of going under, and in this case by chance or by vigilance the awful invisibility was visible enough to be reversed by swift leap and wild grasp and then he was in my arms again,

Whistle, like a newborn gasping and because he is mine, he is mine, he is mine, because on that day he did not die, because my fear from him I try to hide, because in the womb all sound is a kind of music, I started singing.

A POETICS OF SPACE

PREFACE: SHIMMER HERE, SHIMMER

Remember the feel of the latch:
a group of organic habits, such
simple structures. In storm

storm makes sense of shelter.
Imagine living in a seashell,
shrinking enough to be contained.

By clear-eyed words can one
hear oneself close? The rote
of the sea, the roar of, the glint.

1. SIMPLE EXERCISES FOR THE PHENOMENOLOGY OF
   THE IMAGINATION

We begin to dream of nothing in the night.
This, then, is the main problem: to dream
of nothing in the night we are carried back

to the land of motionless childhood. What
a strange thing it is, fossilized duration.
We are never real historians. We once loved

a garret. Was the room a large one?
A matter for the biographer. The biographer
prepares his explosions in the theater of the past

to illustrate an instant's freezing. These
drawings need not be exact. What would be
the use? You would like to tell everything.

I have already said too much. In every country,
a house constitutes a body. Fear in the cellar.
In the attic, rats. The tiniest latch has remained

in our hands: names of things we knew.
Dumas is crying because Dumas has tears.
One very dark night set the waves.

Think of the road this way: what is more
beautiful than a road? Geographers are always
reminding us of an underground horizon.

Such a complicated geometry. Night dreams
just in front of me—of a hut, of a nest,
like an animal in its hole is a distant glimmer.

How many scattered wolves alone before god,
like fireflies, like so many invitations?
Now, still, we could start a new life.

2. THE REVERSE OF THE FUNCTION OF INHABITING

Housewifely, the housewife awakens
reaping an imaginary field. The house-test:
every morning every object a working draft,

a ready-made invitation to the mountains
to come back through the window. Airy
structure, long did I build you in the blue

incense of a red-letter day. A flower
lived where we lived and called it home.
But the question is more complex than that.

The house remodels the man. The cell
of a body having been a refuge
becomes a cyclone. Between the notary

and the heir, the iron hooves of dream
geometry: later, always later, the house
of the future is better, a nest already,

and when you are there you would
like to be. It's always like that.
The gesture of closing is briefer than

that of opening. In the tiniest of hatreds,
an animal filament, a sleeping insect
in its red night. Out the shadow,

show the hatchlings this dove was
a hospitable ark: a winged house
makes good flour from storms.

3. A THEOREM OF INFINITE SPACE

All words do an honest job, the hurried
reader responds in passing. A slight pain,
a mild shock, the rudiments of a story.

This time in little mirrors stopped with sleep
a very white almond appears. Concepts
are drawers not open to just anybody

here and there in the brain, keepsake boxes.
There will always be more things in a closed
than in an open box. What good things are

being kept in reserve, objects friendship,
folded in the russet wood, between the flanks
of the wintry meadow? Objection

overridden, erudite minds lay in provisions,
an anthology of mechanized debates.
On page eighty of the twenty-sixth edition,

you touched what you were touching.
Sufficiently lavendered, under a button,
under a leather tongue, what soft words

cut the story short? Nothing more to
confess, every secret has its little casket.
In other words, a secret is a grave,

a casket is a dungeon as cold as
a police record we should also like to open.
A lock is a threshold, an invitation

to thieves. Well-guarded secret,
slender casket, the lock doesn't exist
that could resist these closing calls.

4. ARCHITECTURE IS THE NATURAL HABITAT OF THE
FUNCTION OF INHABITING

A rat in its hole, a rabbit in its burrow,
cows in the stable. But this is not
our subject. Autumn was there

so there is also an alas in this song.
A nest is a bird's house.
A nest is a hiding place.

An empty nest mocks its finder.
When we discover a nest it takes us back
to our childhood or, rather, to a childhood:

to the childhoods we should have had.
If we return to the old house as to a nest,
it is because memories are dreams.

In order to make so gentle a comparison,
one must have lost the house that stood
for happiness. Values alter facts.

Of the actual nest. We definitely saw it,
but we say that it was well hidden.
The nest we pluck from the hedge

like a dead flower is nothing but a thing.
A legend carries an invisible nest
to its utmost point. The nest is a point

in the atmosphere that always surrounds
large trees. A bird is a worker without tools.
The tree is the vestibule. The nest is

a bouquet. Would a bird build its nest
if it did not have its instinct for confidence
in the world? For the world is a nest.

5. FORM IS THE HABITAT OF LIFE

When the motion picture camera
accelerates the unfolding of a flower,
we receive a sublime image of offering.

Large things can issue from small ones.
The forces of egress are such, the most
dynamic escapes. Shells are

nests from which birds have flown.
Here we have a confusion of genres.
Often when we think we are describing,

we merely imagine. Certain theories
that were once thought to be scientific
are, in reality, boundless daydreams.

Life's principal effort is to make shells.
At the center there was a vast dream of shells.
Inside a man's body is an assemblage of shells.

In the same way there are ambush-houses,
there are trap-shells. There's no need
of a gate, no need of an iron-trimmed door.

For the famished wolf, it is now nothing
but a stone on the road. Amazement
of this kind is rarely felt twice.

Wolves in shells are crueler than stray ones.
Thus a learned daydream collects
legendary hyphens. The russet cuckoo is

simply the gray cuckoo when it is young.
By solving small problems we teach ourselves
to solve large ones. A man, an animal,

an almond—all find maximum repose in a shell.
Place them under the magnifying glass.
We want to see and yet we are afraid to see.

These daydreams are at once long
and brief. We know perfectly well that
to inhabit a shell, we must be alone.

6. THE WORLD IS NOT SO MUCH A NOUN

It is not easy to efface the factors of place:
the point of departure, the germ of the room.
Being becomes manifest at the very moment

it comes forth from its corner.
The child has just discovered that she is
herself. Does she return to her little house?

Words are little houses. Novelists often return
to an invented childhood to recount events
whose naïveté is also invented. The house

preceded the universe. The past is very old.
We recall the hours we have spent in corners.
We find it hard to stop dreaming. An imaginary

room rises up half box, part walls, part door,
like the nest in the tree, like the mollusk.
A little creature fills an empty refuge.

The novelist should have given us the details:
the countless little tools, little thresholds,
the vast museum of insignificant things.

Nothing is ever empty. Each of us has
seen a few lines on the ceiling. The spiral
greeted us with clasped hands.

7. IMAGINATION IN MINIATURE IS NATURAL IMAGINATION

The first microscopic observations were legends.
We must go further. We must believe
ourselves. We have to digest our surprise:

here I am again, little glazed lune, little sun.
To take an exact measure, one must go beyond
logic. Parasol-shaped, this universe is as large

as the other one, exactly the same thing drawn
to different scale. Large issues from small.
There is thus a contradiction in numbers.

Faced with the weak point of the legend,
a reasonable philosopher prepared by
mathematical thoughts asks them to wait

a moment, certain badly camouflaged
rationalizations. Ratty sparrow, the imagination
deserves better than that. The imagination does

not end in a diagram. Seated in the horse's ear—
a wild little knoll, an entire world—one would
like to describe it, the jamming of these waves.

A meadow is a forest, a handful of moss
is a pine wood. A bluebell trembled
like countless others. We haven't time to love

new love when confirming the diagnosis:
the planetary image, the narrow gate,
that little particle of dream.

8. ALL THESE CONSTELLATIONS ARE YOURS

The ship dreams in terms of water.
Beautiful volume, the world stretches out.
Distant sails look like homing pigeons

whose wings once shone blue.
Little by little we take into our lungs
an echo. This is a way of saying

we do not see it start, yet it always starts
in the houses of the past, in the space of
elsewhere. We dream over a map,

desire describing a nation, a desert,
the plain or the plateau, the horizon
as much as the center. In the domain

under consideration, there are no young
forests. Honey in a hive is anything—
white nettle, blue sky. Space starts to dream

in the animal machine. Look in the eyes
of a trembling hare. The instant when
an animal that is all fear becomes lamb-like

calm is a proof: every atlas an absolute
elsewhere, the non-I woods,
the before-us forest.

9. EVERYTHING TAKES FORM

Yes and no, open and closed,
outside and inside. Here and there
the obvious geometry needs mapping.

Banished from the realm, shall we
harden or soften? Language waves,
language bears. Language in danger

utters words that are dangerous.
Then come the nights, hours when
so many doors are closed and all

our former rooms and one's head is
a hive, carries with it bees. What,
do doors open? Does the outside call?

Hesitation: a threshold god,
a two-way dream. Reversals even of
imaginary projects suppose a grasp.

First of all, who invites us? Philosophies
want principles, rules immediately
become clear. One has only to

aggravate the line—begin by admiring,
by exaggerating the habits
of a fine example. How concrete

everything becomes between parentheses:
a chaplet, a refrain, so much talk.
Too many things in the false light

I have wanted. Intimacy can be
shut in, its tiny fibers upset by a word
exchange their dizziness: dovetailing

thoughts unwelded. There is no need
to return to the highly colored heart.
The cell of the secret is white.

10. ON THE SUBJECT OF SCIENTIFIC THINKING

Intimate data, speak briefly. A walnut
in its shell bears the mark of a tree
in its meadow straining toward god

in countless green spheres: the round
cry of round, like a cupola the rounded
dome of sky, the roundness of a mouth

broken with every kind of thunder.
A bird is a round life. Everything round
invites a caress, the arrow figures,

full of accidents twinkling. A young lawyer
would love to know which ones. Is this
the moment? The author doesn't say.

The author has failed to recognize another
horizon handed over too vivid is empty.
Such data, if we must take them,

we must take for ourselves alone.
Doublet dreams and thoughts reply
but they do not tell us everything.

The walnut tree lives in a different register.
The bird is the same. This is how:
absolute bird, live ball guarded on all sides.

WHERE THE USE OF CANNON IS IMPRACTICAL

Stranger, mislaid love, I will
sleepwalk all night not girlish
but zombie-like, zombie-lite
through the streets in search of
your arms. Let's meet at dawn
in the park to practice an ancient art
while people roll by in the latest
space-age gear blank as mirrors
above the procedure in the stainless-
steel theaters where paper-gowned
we take ourselves to take ourselves
apart. Tap-tap-spark. So little blazes.
Cover the roofs with precision hooves.
Push back the forest like a blanket.
A bird the right color is invisible,
only movement catches the eye.
My most illustrious Lord, I know
how to remove water from moats
and how to make an infinite number
of bridges. Here we are at the palace.
Here we are in the dark, dark woods.

SHOT THROUGH

In Hollywood, it looks like this:
sped up, slowed down, eerily
fallen over. You wake with
a needle in your arm, a spider
in the soup of the blood, a doctor
rebandaging your ripped-up wrists.
No matter how kindly the face,
there's no fix for this. Time
had a beginning. Wouldn't that
be nice? A movie just waiting to
be made. Everyone else's fingers
stroke smoothly their chosen spines,
but not mine. Let's say this is
temporary. In the fire we know
the sun. Some particles do in fact
escape. The littlest has done it.
Look at the lap she sits in now.
In this vortex we are the chaos
crumbs, the sparks peeling off.
Falling cold. That's a long story.
No matter what, the assistant is
always the most beleaguered one.
She fought it. I nursed her.
Of course I loved her. I thought
it would alleviate my own situation.
This tent, a flimsy idea, became
our home. These liberties we took.
We take. Let's try.

SO LONG

Mother falcon beautifully
arranged on your shit-stained
sill, stilled for the incubation
under a camera's monocular eye
so that we may pry, bullet-bird
golden-lidded, we should let you
sleep instead of watching you try.
Hover-blink-repeat. Update:
you moved a muscle. Update:
the air swept down. Update:
you've trailed back some blood
on your beak from last night's
thrill. How many pills to kill
this thin papery feeling? More,
or, as yet not enough. Trafficked
arms, rapacious tongue, greedy
gullet, enough is a matter of much
debate. Mother, you are late.
I ate the glinting of your hair,
your knuckle in the steaming soup.
You bled into me just like now
into the ground we beat these wings.

ACHILLES REALLY LOVED THAT GIRL

Leave me to it, let me have it,
where the fuck have you been?
Orange-lipped moon, oriole's
enflamed breast, did you see it
blah, blah, blah? Sing for—sing so—
singed eyebrows and forearms
from the funny little explosion,
baby's favorite party trick,
watch me now. Lean in a little
closer. I like your blouse or maybe
it's that I like your body in it.
To tell the truth, I lie a little,
add a few here, take a few there.
Good fortune next to bad is
awkward, unseemly, but good
next to good loses some of its
luster, doesn't it? Professor,
I mean, Lisa, I mean, hey girl,
I found the work kind of weak,
maybe, a bit unconvincing.
I felt like the author was always
letting herself off the hook,
like maybe it needed a longer
runway, I mean, I could always
tell where the drift was heading.

RUN EVERY RACE AS IF IT'S YOUR LAST

As you round the bend
keep the steel and mouse-skinned
rabbit front left center
and the track and the crowd
and its cries are a blurred ovation
as you stumble and recover
and then fully fall even if
only onto the rough gravel
of your inside mind or outside
in what is called the real world
as how many drunken grandfathers
holding little girls' hands
and broken peanut shells go
swirling by. Why are you racing?
What are you racing from?
From what fixed arm does this
moth-eaten rabbit run?
Captive is different than stupid.
Near dead is different than dead.
They call it a decoy but we know
a mirror when we see ourselves
lurch and dive for one.

CONSIDER YOURSELVES ALL "DEBBIE"

Dear Debbie, why is it so hard
to understand? The accident was
me. It was in me, it was on me,
it keeps getting written all over
my face. Watch your tongue,
you might say, or, go ahead
and fix your face. But help is
on the other side, Debbie,
my good one, it's stuck in profile,
Debbie, it's not on its way.
Use our arms as your arms,
the ditch lilies beckon. There,
they say, now you know what it's like
to be pleasantly ignored. We keep
all the wrong appointments,
Debbie. Sunday bleeds into Monday
and unlike flowers, Monday
will not be ignored. Because.
Because. Because, Debbie,
Monday is ugly and awkward
and never knows what you really
just don't want to hear. Because
Monday is the last person
you want to see right now
but there she is again. Because
time is a wheel, Debbie. Because
I am Monday and Monday is this
accident, Debbie. How many times
do I have to tell you?

READY REGRET

She used the stadium. I would have
chosen the bridge. We're not even
Division One. Our tailgate crowds are
mostly enthusiastic about beer.
Sunlight in the trees. Sunlight
in the trees. I thought these feelings
would be blonder, like that virus
that doesn't kill you but kills
in you what tells you to wake up.
All the good and bad souls who
size me up judge a different woman
from the one you used to know:
two-room apartment with a view
of cold as imagined by lack of snow,
nut-and-honey cookies for three weeks
only to entice the spring and later
year-round because we can't wait
for anything anymore so we forget what
the sweetness was supposed to mean.

YOUR COUNTRY NEEDS YOU

Maybe one time standing
behind a lectern you heard voices
and realized they were what
your own mouth just said and quickly
you grew accustomed to giving orders.
Or maybe standing there you said
nothing at all and the next thing
you knew some night-shift nurse
of the invisibly wounded was
monitoring your fitful dreams.
Like everyone, I'll watch indefinitely
while the meant-to-be lovers stay
a lip's-width apart or a war zone,
their shadows overlapping like animals
around a dried-up watering hole.
I keep expecting someone prettier
when I look in the mirror. See
how we shatter then reassemble
as I turn away back into the day.

CHARISMATIC MEGAFAUNA

Fruit of the vine, fish on
the line, chip on the shoulder,
off the old—not far from
the tree. The cops found Caesar
when they broke up the party.
The landlord found Circe
when he cleared the place out.
The zoo finds tires for each
to paw and a hose to stream.
Nature says grassland-acres-ibex.
Nurture says asphalt-kibble-fence.
The sun says sleep, sleep, O my
America, O my newfound land.
These ones we care about
because we gave them names.

PIONEER ME

Welcome to the museum.
Did you come after work
on poor middle-class
half-priced half-an-hour night?
The face-blind painter works
for decades on his own likeness.
He calls everyone doll, as in
baby, as in baby, the heat of
your skin is the flipped switch
that turns this whole place on.
Here, take this chair. Quiet
now, let me leave you by
the window where I've broken
this stick in two over you,
across the lake of your face:
no more June, there's something
blue-hued and sinking now
beneath the skin, endlessly pinned,
a river returning. The bank is
the bedside. Glitter-spilled stars
velvet the gaze. Go ahead,
be the change I want to make.
Let me undress you down to
the plainest beige sail you
become, something hovering like
the meadow above the meadow,
like the dirt when it hums.

THEN THEY ATE THEIR HORSES

Every so many seconds a bomb
goes off, a car veers, a needle enters.
Every so many seconds a murmur
somewhere in a tunnel collapsing.
Once the liquid womb, now
a different ocean pressing.
Reverse it, put back the blood
on the inside of skin, call back
the blooming skirts, sweep the throat
clean of everything but its whisper.
Some stories won't be told no matter
how many words settle the land of us,
no matter how many birds come
to steal the seeds. Swab the pickax
gently around me. I had a bad dream.
How many men fit into this ditch
beside me? What color before were
my robes? Look, my cuffs are golden.
My sleeves, all along, they were red.

THE CANARY'S JOB IS TO DIE

little flame
little match struck
little sunspot
little filament
golden smudge
silent siren
of no more air
of no longer there
suddenly fled we flee
go ahead and try
go ahead and die

THE SYMPTOM POOL

Even in death a herd animal
doesn't like to go it alone
so around and around the field
the dead horse goes until there
are two, three, four to travel
together. Enter a certain weather.
Fall of failing and of failing
to see it through. Enter birds
starting up unmercifully in the dark
and the nonstop whirring of
the little machine you call heart.
Enter the copycat hallway, the same
caliber loaded grandfather's gun,
the ball bearings and black backpacks
exploding in the sun. Enter this
season's dresses fanning out
in mermaid tails so all the girls'
legs look pegged on below
the knee. Enter legs pegged on
below the knee, the bewildered
girlfriend, the shutdown capitol,
the sweet stench of uneaten hay.

PEOPLE ARE HANGED CURTAINS ARE HUNG

Hunger returns before our ability
to digest. Digestion begins
in the mouth, a chorus of
let's say hurricanes, let's say
wolves. Questions rise
with their answers beside them,
histories given in hospitals,
in bedrooms to which we no longer
belong. I do want to take back
control of my life. I didn't know
my deceased grandmother had
an account in both of our names.
I am looking for a fresh start
like the tiger set free from
the royal zookeeper's private
dressing room weeks after the siege
into a world of still no food.

UNKNOWN BELOVED

The canopy is singing.
Sloths in sleep look like the dreaming
dead. Awake little different
under eyelashes stalwart as sapodillas,
fringed as palms. If to attain true mastery
ten thousand hours are required, yes.
If it is the habit of geniuses to nap,
yes. If the highly successful sleep
fewer than four hours per night,
the inverse. If expert survivalists sleep
while maintaining partial consciousness,
the reverse. But we sleep fitful in a bed
at the average, appointed intervals
and under it we keep only some number
of heaped-up words. What is our dreaming
good for, it is reasonable to wonder,
in what are we expert? A certain fumbling
in the hours when we make good
habitats for other organisms, which is
where first we recognized each other.

BLUE STRAGGLERS

I can't compete with your wizardry
or that gold comb in your hair.
Your packed lunches involve cherries
and other provisions precisely laid
as only a sea captain might command
and never be asked to share. Sometimes
it's a question of scale: a raspberry
to the lip, a horse's muzzle to the palm.
Sometimes it's a question of distance:
mercury threads of geese five miles high,
the sky a sink and our bravest journeys
the quiver that escapes a broken thermometer
chased by a child's thumb. We'd be lying
if we didn't acknowledge that a playmate's
tumble is a good opportunity to seize
the ball on its lazy roll away. Why not
admire the vulture? The eagle scavenges,
too, and its wing beat is no more or less
magnificent. Knowledge is temperamental,
like how I sat for all those hours in French
class while people grew fluent around me
and I learned only the rote conjugation
of a few useless verbs, but I can recall every
brown fleck that littered your green eyes.
Here, I wove you this poncho out of gentian
petals using only a junco's beak. Gently,
I shoehorn my dreams each night into bed,
but even they drift off and in the end
only this half-baked heartbreak is mine.

CINDERS OF

Never before have I found airplanes
or the blinking red eyes of hundred-story
cranes so beautiful, L.A. People
eating and drinking and glowing
in hot tubs on rooftops under a few
persistent stars and the silver bodies of
steel origami jets ashing like lit cigarettes
as they sweep languid across the lapis sky.
End of the century is what the scientists say
today, give or take, less. Already we are
in excess. Was it Galileo who dreamt
of a fine-masted ship meant by wind
to explore the heavens? Home, how long
have we longed to leap from you, to return?
A humming colony, inside the plane
we breathe obediently our modicum
of bottled air, choiceless, blameless
for decisions made by now so long ago
back on the ground. We would all take more
than our share, but when one among us
cries out, those nearest quickly attend,
the rest stand by, stand guard, we like to
pretend, stand up, stand tall, stand down.
How differently will the moment construe
itself across the screens of our faces later when
once more we tell a story called I Survived.
I'd like to report a woman raving in the street.
I'd like to report a man with no shoes
sleeping on a grate at the corner of Figueroa
and Ninth. I'd like to report a gun in a holster
on a hip in my classroom, a person with
a deadly weapon whose intent I cannot
determine. I'd like to report a desperate hope.
I'd like to report too little, too late. I'd like

to report the newspaper of record. I'd like to
report the victim's family has not yet been
notified. We are gathered here today
in the cinders of pumas wearing Pumas
on rooftops and red-eyes in and out of L.A.
Jellyfish will inherit the earth. We've learned
to despise anything invasive, but everyone loves
a winner. I mean, they may keep their curtain
closed, but first class would turn to us in a heartbeat,
in a pinch. Let's say someone needed to be
tackled or something malfunctioned and for once
back here there was more air. We wouldn't
hold it against them. Last night on the street
beneath a bullet like this one I drank in a life
story because I was thirsty. I shared one
because I was asked. This, too, was a version
of the conversation we keep needing
not to let ourselves have.

Notes

"The Disaster" and "Turned Back the Disaster Comes Back" collage phrases from Maurice Blanchot's *The Writing of the Disaster.*

"What We're Trying to Do Is Create a Community of Dreamers" uses as source material comments by Hunter Lee Soik as quoted in "Dream On," in the October 28, 2013, issue of the *New Yorker.*

Each section of "A Poetics of Space" uses a corresponding chapter of Gaston Bachelard's *The Poetics of Space* as a source text.

Several poems borrow or riff upon phrases by others: *The messengers come when you are sitting at the table,* Joy Williams; *My muse is not a horse,* Nick Cave; *Love never dies a natural death,* Anaïs Nin; *One case from [the] past is cause for particular vexation,* Anthony Lane; *Where the use of cannon is impractical* and *My most illustrious Lord, I know how to remove water...,* Leonardo da Vinci; *Here we are at the palace...* and *We mourn the end by applauding,* Sarah Ruhl; *How many pills to kill this thin papery feeling,* Sylvia Plath; *O my America, O my newfound land,* John Donne.

ACKNOWLEDGMENTS

Thank you to the editors of the journals, anthologies, and sites where poems from this book first appeared: the Academy of American Poets' Poem-a-Day, *The Ampersand Review, The Awl, Bat City Review, Birdfeast, The Book of Scented Things* (Literary House Press), *Boston Review, Columbia: A Journal of Literature & Art, Columbia Poetry Review, Conduit,* Connotation Press, *Gulf Coast, Handsome, Into Quarterly, Linebreak, Matter: A (Somewhat) Monthly Journal of Political Poetry and Commentary, Narrative,* PEN America Poetry Series, *Prairie Schooner, A Public Space, Southern Humanities Review, Still Life with Poem* (Literary House Press), *Washington Square Review,* and *Whole Terrain.*

Many thanks to Shane McCrae for selecting the poems constituting the third section of this book for the Essay Press Chapbook Contest Series and to the editors of Essay Press for publishing them under the title *The Resemblance of the Enzymes of Grasses to Those of Whales Is a Family Resemblance.*

Love and thanks to Heather Abel, Suzanne Buffam, Kris Delmhorst, Noy Holland, Elizabeth McCracken, Jane Miller, Srikanth Reddy, Betsy Wheeler, and Dean Young for their encouragement and suggestions; to Erika Blumenfeld for her exquisite work and permission to use some of it here; to Michael Wiegers and everyone at Copper Canyon Press for their passion and expertise; to the friends who keep company in and around these poems; to my family for the sustenance of their love and support; and to David for making it all possible.

ABOUT THE AUTHOR

Lisa Olstein is the author of three previous poetry collec-
tions: *Radio Crackling, Radio Gone,* winner of the Hayden
Carruth Award, *Lost Alphabet,* a *Library Journal* best book
of the year selection, and *Little Stranger,* named a top book
of the year by *Coldfront.* She is the recipient of a Pushcart
Prize, a Lannan Writing Residency, and an Essay Press
chapbook prize, as well as fellowships from the Sustainable
Arts Foundation, the Massachusetts Cultural Council, and
Centrum. She is a member of the poetry faculty at the
University of Texas, Austin.

Poetry is vital to language and living. Since 1972, Copper Canyon Press has published extraordinary poetry from around the world to engage the imaginations and intellects of readers, writers, booksellers, librarians, teachers, students, and donors.

WE ARE GRATEFUL FOR THE MAJOR SUPPORT PROVIDED BY:

THE PAUL G. ALLEN
FAMILY FOUNDATION

Lannan

The Chinese character for poetry is made up of two parts:
"word" and "temple." It also serves as pressmark for
Copper Canyon Press.

The poems are set in News Gothic.
Printed on archival-quality paper.
Book design and composition by Phil Kovacevich.